Rosa M. Curto

Draw the Magic Fairy

Draw the Magic Blue Fairy

Enslow Elementary
an imprint of
Enslow Publishers, Inc.
40 Industrial Road
Box 398
Berkeley Heights, NJ 07922
USA

http://www.enslow.com

Delicious Cakes

Draw cakes in only three steps!

The blue fairy bakes soft, delicious cakes.

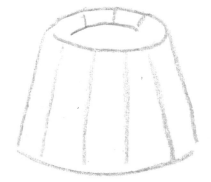

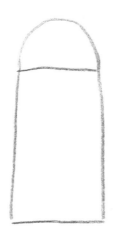
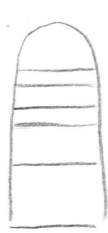

Here are six different cakes you can draw.
You can make many more.

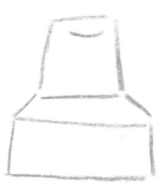

Slices of Cake

Draw a triangle and rectangle to make a slice of cake.

The blue fairy loves sweets!

4

You can draw a piece of cake from any point of view. Decorate the pieces any way you like.

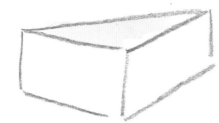

Now you can use two rectangles and a triangle to draw more slices of cake.

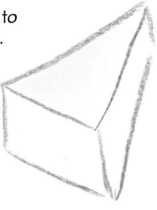

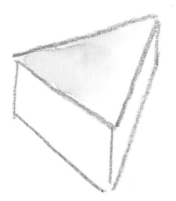

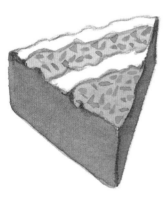

The blue fairy loves to throw parties and serve cake!

Kitchenware

A gourd becomes a bottle.

A leaf becomes a plate.

6

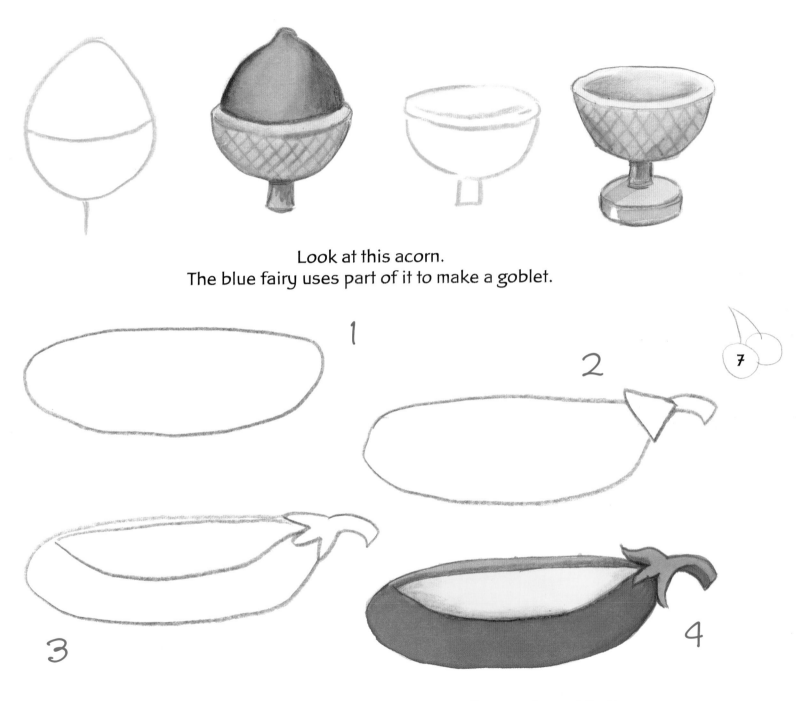

Look at this acorn.
The blue fairy uses part of it to make a goblet.

1

2

7

3

4

An empty eggplant can be used to store smaller seeds and fruits.
It can also be used as a tray.

Cup and Jug

1

Start drawing the cup
with a simple trapezoid.

2

Add an oval
to the top.

3

Round off
the trapezoid.

4

Draw two
curved lines.

5

Draw some leaves
for decoration.

6

Finish the details.

7

Paint it any way you wish.

This is a cup for the blue fairy.

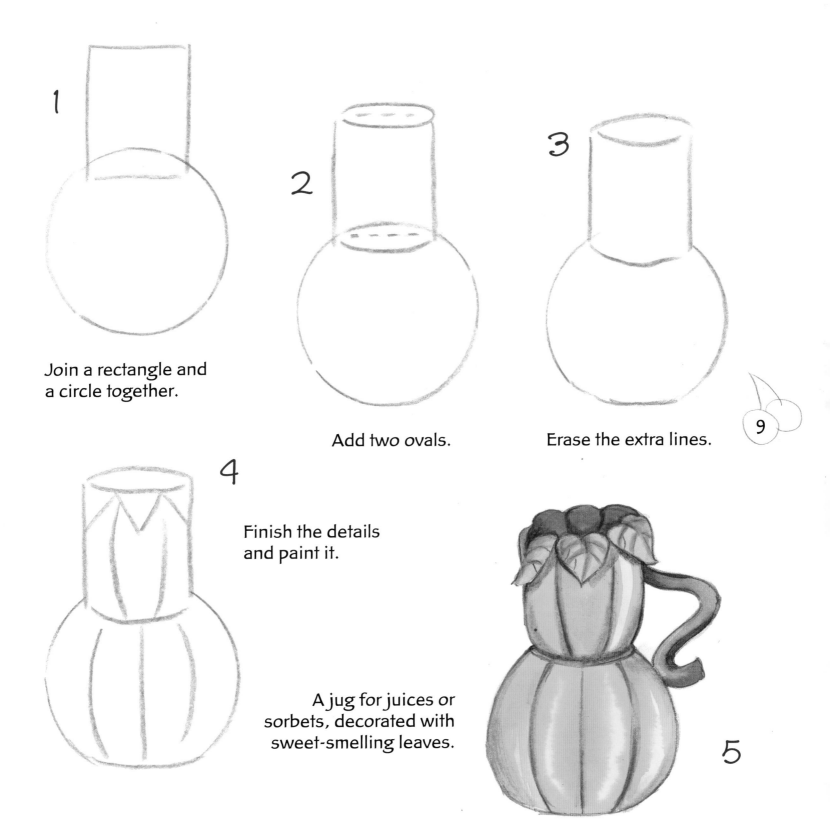

1

Join a rectangle and
a circle together.

2

Add two ovals.

3

Erase the extra lines.

9

4

Finish the details
and paint it.

A jug for juices or
sorbets, decorated with
sweet-smelling leaves.

5

Moving Leaves

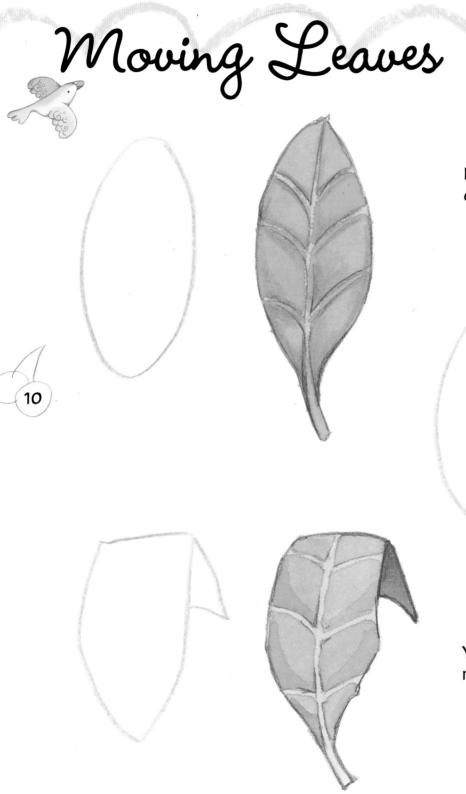

No two leaves are
exactly the same.

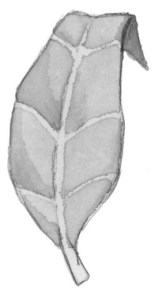

You can bend the tip of the leaf,
making folds of different sizes.

You can also
curl them, either
at the ends or
along both sides.

The leaves twist, bend,
and turn.
Find some leaves to look
at as examples.

Follow only two steps to draw a leaf!

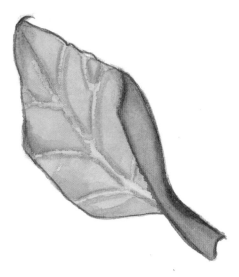

Good Fruit

Fruit helps us stay healthy.
It also gives us energy.

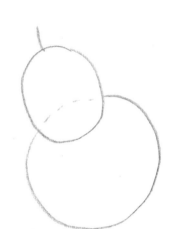

Fruit contains the vitamins
our bodies need to work.

12

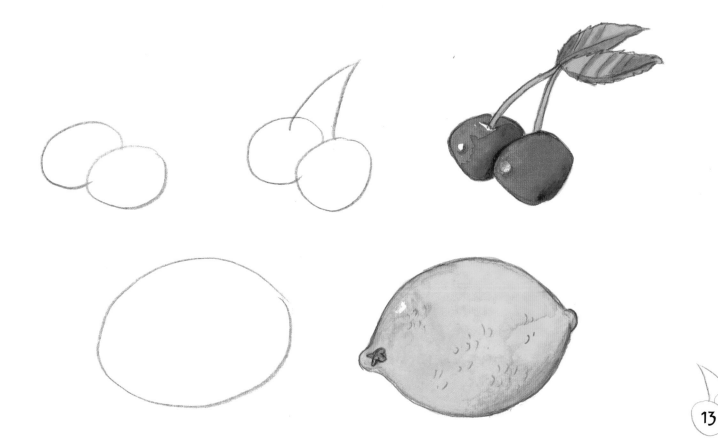

13

The blue fairy and her friends make their magic elixirs from fruit.

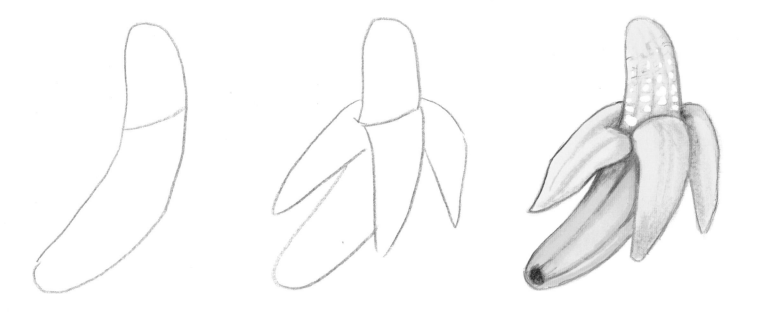

Colorful Butterflies

Fairies can change size when they need to.
Sometimes they are as small as butterflies.

Then they blend in with them.
You have to look carefully!

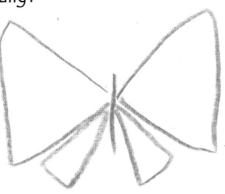

Simon the Squirrel

1 Draw two circles.

2 Draw some simple little hands.

3 Add the feet.

Outline the tail and the ears. **4**

5 Round off the drawing.

6 Paint it.

16

1

Now you can draw Simon from another angle.

2

3

Cute and cuddly...

4

17

Simon collects nuts and acorns. He is a great friend to the blue fairy. He is very playful and a great jumper.

5

6

Birds With Golden Beaks

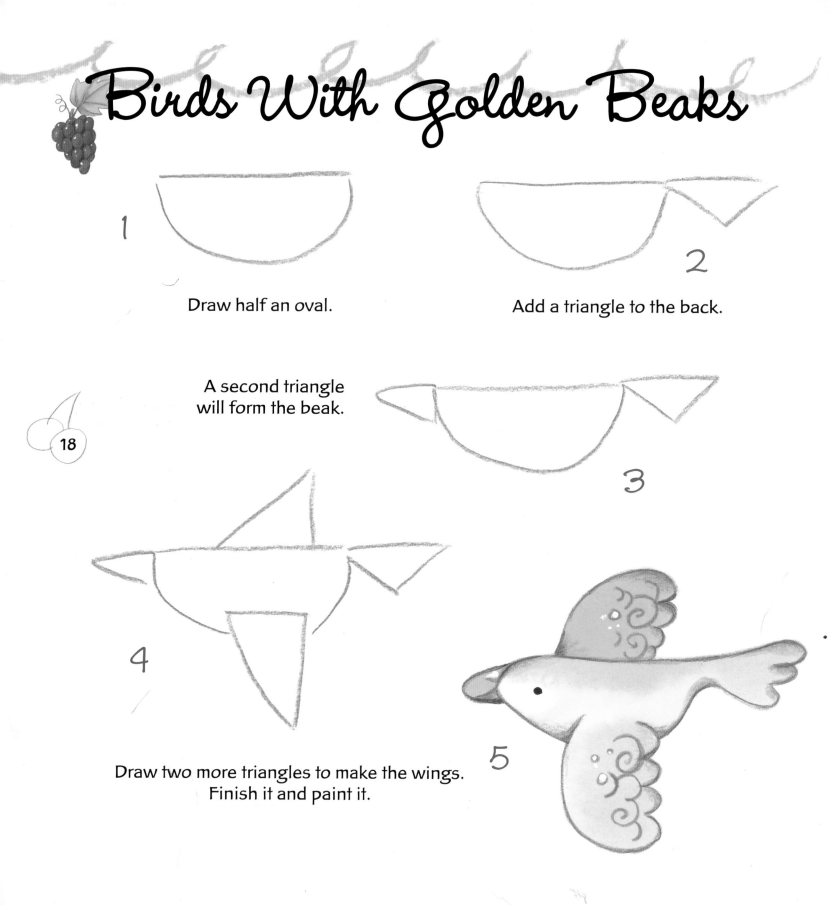

1

Draw half an oval.

2

Add a triangle to the back.

A second triangle
will form the beak.

3

4

Draw two more triangles to make the wings.
Finish it and paint it.

5

18

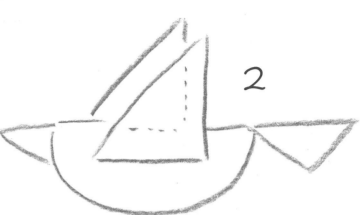

1

You can place the wings in a different position to make a second bird.

2

3

Birds are very fast. They carry fairies from one place to another when the fairies' wings are tired or hurt. Birds help the fairies until they are completely rested or healed.

19

Their feathers are very soft.

4

Different Hairstyles

Fairies can have loose or bunched-up hair. Their hair can be blonde or brown or any color. They like to decorate their hair with fruit or flowers.

Fairy hairstyles come in all different shapes and colors.

The fairies like to look pretty!

When you draw the fairies, maybe you can come up with special hairstyles of your own.

Clothing and Accessories

Most fairies make their clothes themselves from leaves and flower petals.

Love

Light

Dreams

Magic wands: There is a different one for each spell.

Necklaces, bracelets, and headbands
are made out of berries.

The Blue Fairy

1

Start with a circle
and two trapezoids.

2

The trapezoids are the
blouse and skirt.
Draw triangles for sleeves.

Outline the hair,
the neck, the arms,
and the hands.

3

Add the legs and feet.

4

24

Finish the arms and legs.

5

Add the wings.

6

Finish the details and paint her.

7

If you would like to find the blue fairy, look for her among the flowers.

Fairy Amy

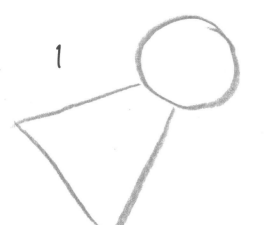

1

Draw a circle and a trapezoid.

2

Add a smaller trapezoid for the neck.

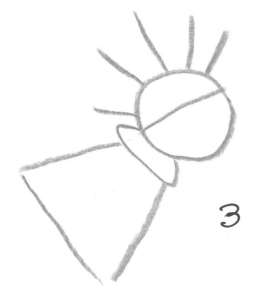

3

Draw lines for the hair.

Draw a sleeve, an arm, and the legs.

4

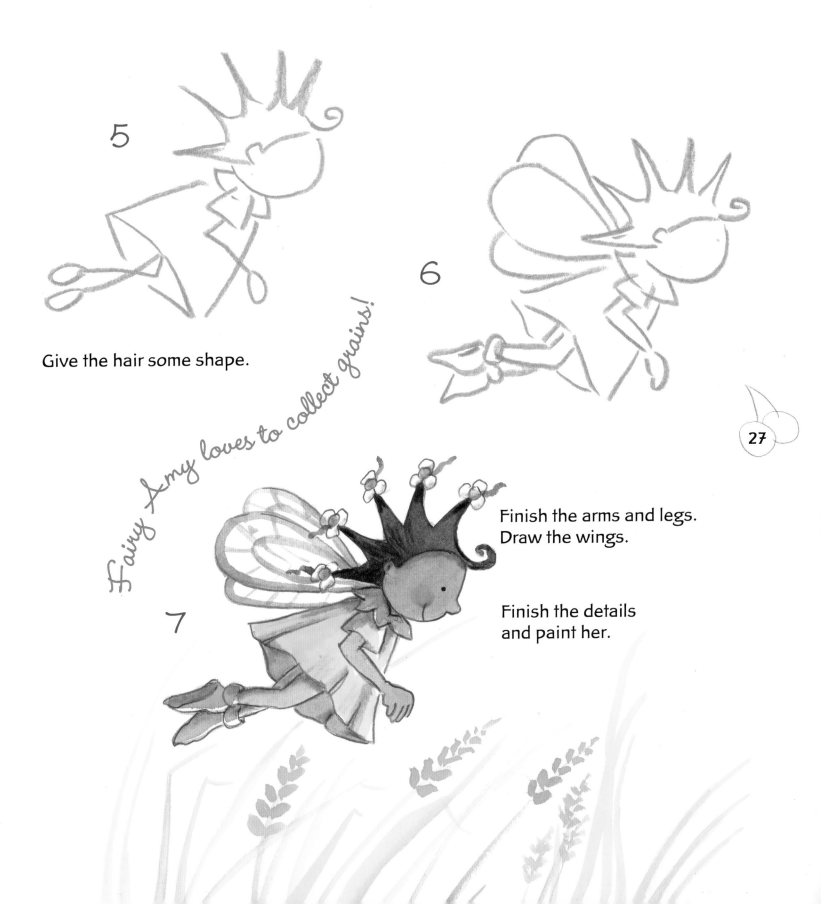

5

Give the hair some shape.

6

Fairy Amy loves to collect grains!

27

7

Finish the arms and legs.
Draw the wings.

Finish the details
and paint her.

Fairy Emily

1 Start with a circle, a trapezoid, and a rectangle.

2 Add a triangle for the wing.

3 Outline the arms and legs.

4 Round off the shapes and draw the second wing.

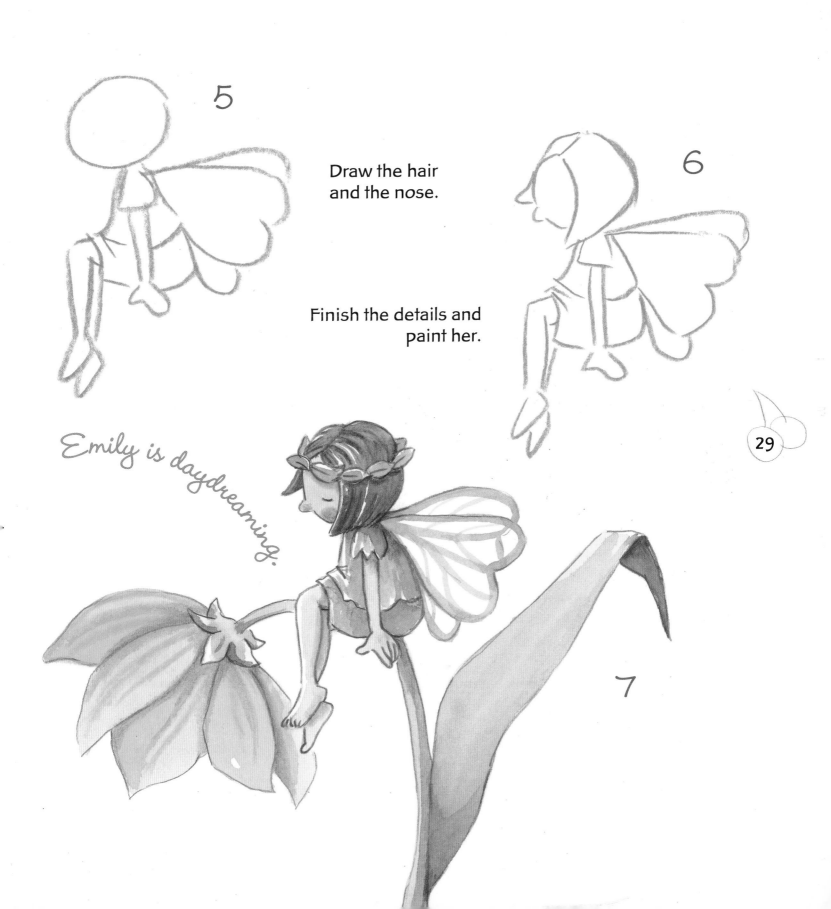

5

Draw the hair and the nose.

6

Finish the details and paint her.

Emily is daydreaming.

7

Fairy Rachel

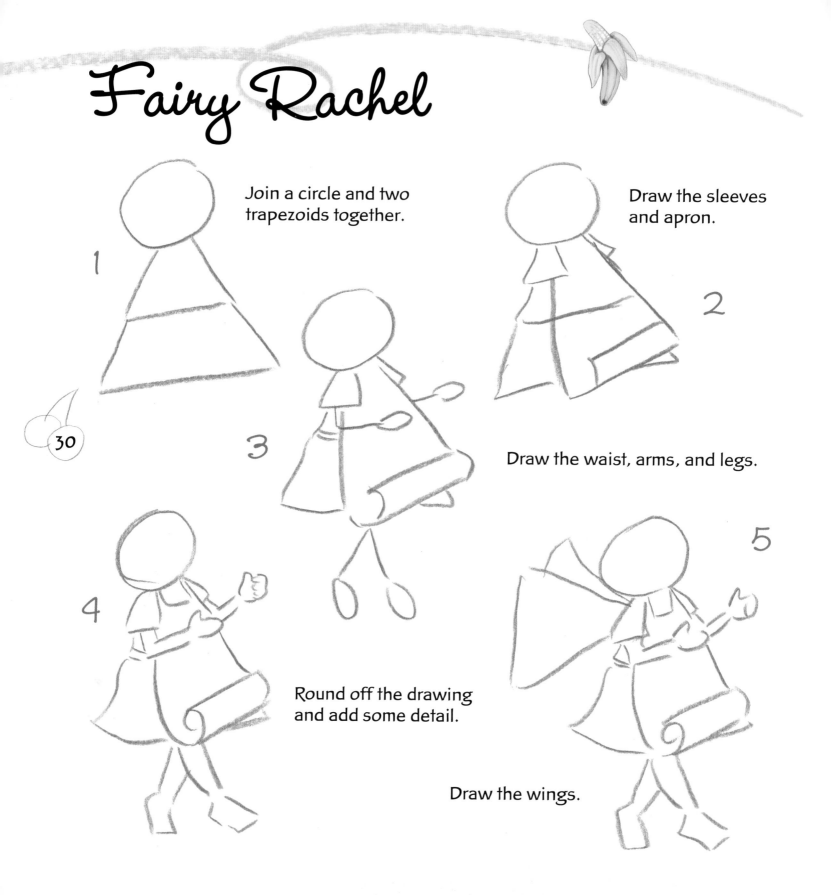

Join a circle and two trapezoids together.

1

Draw the sleeves and apron.

2

30

3

Draw the waist, arms, and legs.

4

Round off the drawing and add some detail.

5

Draw the wings.

6

Add a hat and
some detail on
the apron.

7

Finish off the shapes and
add volume to them.
Finally, add the face and
paint her.

Her favourite flowers are violets.

8

Look Carefully

Take an apple and turn it around slowly while looking at it the whole time.
Place it in different positions.
Put it on a table and move it.
Look at it from the front, the side, upside down...
Draw it, keeping in mind its rounded shape.

Which angle do you like best?

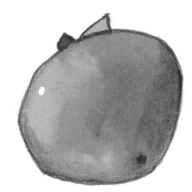
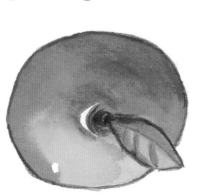

Take a strawberry, the apple, and a kiwi.
First, look at the shapes of these three pieces of fruit.
Then cut them in half and draw them.

The insides look interesting.

33

We find new shapes and colours.

Play and Learn

Far and Near

Look at some trees from a distance and draw them.
You will see the overall shapes and colors, but not the details.

Try it!

Now look very closely
at just one tree.
Draw a branch with
its leaves.

Do you see all the veins, spots, and folds?

Enslow Elementary, an imprint of Enslow Publishers, Inc.
Enslow Elementary® is a registered trademark of Enslow Publishers, Inc.

Original title of the book in Catalan: *DIBUIXANT EL MÓN DE LES FADES 1*
Copyright © GEMSER PUBLICATIONS, S.L., 2012
C/ Castell, 38; Teià (08329) Barcelona, Spain (World Rights)
Tel: 93 540 13 53
E-mail: info@mercedesros.com
Web site: http://www.mercedesros.com
Author and illustrator: Rosa Maria Curto

Library of Congress Cataloging-in-Publication Data

Curto, Rosa Maria.
  [Dibuixant el món de les fades. 1. English]
  Draw the magic blue fairy / Rosa M. Curto.
    pages cm — (Draw the magic fairy)
  Summary: "Learn how to draw the world of the blue fairy, including her other fairy friends, different animals, food, clothes, hairstyles, and much more"—Provided by publisher.
  ISBN 978-0-7660-4265-0
  1. Drawing—Technique—Juvenile literature. 2. Fairies in art—Juvenile literature. I. Title.
  NC655.C8713 2013
  741.2—dc23
                        2012030380

Future edition:
Paperback ISBN 978-1-4644-0473-3

Printed in China
122012 Leo Paper Group, Heshan City, Guangdong, China
10 9 8 7 6 5 4 3 2 1